# IT'S OUR NATURE

Text by **REBECA OROZCO**

Illustrated by **MENENA COTTIN**

**TUNDRA BOOKS**

© Ediciones Tecolote, 2008, Arca de valores. Original edition in Spanish.
© Rebeca Orozco
© Menena Cottin

Authorized English edition for North America © Tundra Books, 2012
English translation copyright © 2012 by Tamara Sztainbok

Published in Canada by Tundra Books, a division of Random House of Canada
Limited, One Toronto Street, Suite 300, Toronto, Ontario M5C 2V6

Published in the United States by Tundra Books of Northern New York,
P.O. Box 1030, Plattsburgh, New York 12901

Library of Congress Control Number: 2011938779

www.tundrabooks.com

**Library and Archives Canada Cataloguing in Publication**

Orozco, Rebeca

    It's our nature / by Rebeca Orozco ; illustrated by Menena Cottin.

Translation of: Arca de valores.
ISBN 978-1-77049-283-7

    1. Animals – Juvenile literature.  I. Cottin, Menena  II. Title.

QL49.O7613 2012       j590       C2011-906512-6

We acknowledge the financial support of the Government of Canada through the
Canada Book Fund and that of the Government of Ontario through the Ontario
Media Development Corporation's Ontario Book Initiative. We further acknowledge the support of the Canada Council for the Arts and the Ontario Arts Council
for our publishing program.

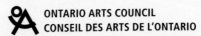

Printed and bound in China

1 2 3 4 5 6      17 16 15 14 13 12

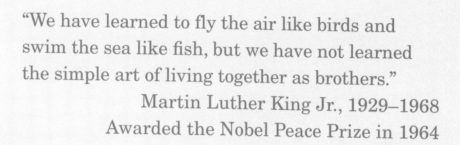

"We have learned to fly the air like birds and swim the sea like fish, but we have not learned the simple art of living together as brothers."
Martin Luther King Jr., 1929–1968
Awarded the Nobel Peace Prize in 1964

We have a lot in common with animals. We experience love, pain, happiness, and sorrow. Animals do too. We share these feelings and others as well. But animals could show us a thing or two about responsibility, community, generosity, and tolerance.

Maybe it's time for animals to teach us a few tricks! Read on to find out what we can learn from our animal friends.

# HOWLER MONKEY
## Altruism

In the canopy of a tree, the howler monkey hangs from a branch. Hearing the steps of a jaguar on the undergrowth, he floods the forest with howling to frighten the intruder. When the jaguar does not turn back, the howler monkey changes the volume of his call to alert his troop to the danger.

The howler monkey chooses to save his companions before himself. Thanks to his warning cry, the females are able to escape with their babies, and the males defend the troop by throwing fruit and branches at the enemy. Finally, the jaguar retreats and the monkeys are safe.

# FLAMINGO
## Community

Births are a time of happiness. When the flamingo chick breaks through the shell, her excited parents flap their wings and go into a frenzy to feed and care for her. Looking after a new chick is exhausting! By the end of the week, the parents need a break. They fly to the lake to rest and feed.

They take the little flamingo to a part of the lake where a group of parents, a sort of daycare, look after all the chicks. The next day, another group of flamingos will care for the babies so that their fellow flamingos can rest.

# DOLPHIN
## Communication

The first thing the little dolphin sees when he is born is an enormous figure next to him. It is his mother. Softly and sweetly, the mother whistles in the baby's ear to pass along the art of communication. She helps him learn to recognize her voice and to develop his own personal whistle. In the same way a human voice or fingerprint is unique, the dolphin's whistle is his own, different from any other dolphin's whistle.

# ELEPHANT
## Generosity

The hungry little elephant searches for his mother. He can't find her. She has moved away from the herd to feed and rest.

For a moment, the little elephant feels lost. But other elephant mothers arrive and nurse him. The little elephant drinks all the milk he wants and runs off to explore. He is surrounded by younger female elephants that protect him from harm – they are used to caring for the youngest of the herd. It's good practice for when they have their own babies to look after!

# ARMADILLO
## Responsibility

The armadillo mother spends long hours with her four children. She teaches them to catch ants and termites to eat, to dig deep tunnels to protect themselves, and to flatten piles of dried leaves to clear a path.

Just as a snake is about to attack, the mother
uses her armor in defense and the little ones
imitate her. They are all unharmed!

The mother is proud of her offspring. She has
prepared them to face the world's dangers.

# CROCODILE
## Trust

On the shores of a river, tiny crocodiles break through their shells and emerge into the world for the first time.

When the mother takes the baby crocodiles
to the pond, she carefully transports them in
her mouth.

In the water, the newborns search for insects
and little fish to eat. When they hear the
growl of a wild animal, they quickly swim to
the one place they know they will be safe –
their mother's enormous mouth!

# OCTOPUS
## Commitment

In an underwater cave, the female octopus cares for her 150,000 eggs. She makes sure that they are clean and receive plenty of oxygen. She also protects them from enemies.

She is so dedicated to her eggs that she does not leave the cave for three months, not even for a second! Even when food appears within reach of her tentacles, she pays it no attention – she continues to care for her eggs.

When the time comes for the babies to be born, they break through their eggs. The mother, like her ancestors before her, dies from weakness.

# PENGUIN
## Solidarity

At dawn, a mother penguin lays her egg.
Exhausted, she leaves it with her mate
and goes out to sea to find food for her chick
and herself.

The male accepts the egg and keeps it from
touching the frozen ground. He places it on his
feet and covers it with his feathers.

To protect themselves against the wind and
the cold, the males huddle together to form
a circle. Taking turns, those who have been
on the outside of the circle move into the
center of the group where it is warmer,
while the penguins on the inside move to
the outskirts.

Two months pass before the mother
returns with food. She arrives just in
time to witness the birth of her chick.

# WOLF
## Brotherhood

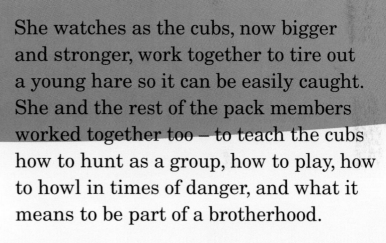

The mother wolf remembers how her newborn cubs eagerly drank her milk. There were three of them – one male and two females. Their eyes were only half open, their ears were small, and they moved clumsily.

She watches as the cubs, now bigger and stronger, work together to tire out a young hare so it can be easily caught. She and the rest of the pack members worked together too – to teach the cubs how to hunt as a group, how to play, how to howl in times of danger, and what it means to be part of a brotherhood.

# WILDEBEEST
## Tolerance

A violent wind blows up dust.
The dry season is beginning.
For the million and a half
wildebeests that live on the
savanna, the time has come
to head for the cool grasslands.

Zebras, gazelles, and buffalos are also migrating hundreds of miles in search of water. Groups of hungry lions and hyenas follow, hoping to find some prey to hunt.

To improve their chances of survival, the zebras mix in with the wildebeests. The wildebeests accept them into the group and continue walking by their side on the long journey to find water.

In the grasslands, the forests, the deserts, and the seas, animals learn to get along. They tolerate each other's differences and embrace diversity.

We are part of the same animal kingdom. We can learn to live in harmony with each other and the world around us too!